W0018886

Lots of Lemons

Anne Taylor

Seed Learning

Top Phonics Readers 1
Lots of Lemons

Anne Taylor

© 2017 Seed Learning, Inc.

Acquisitions Editor: Rose Morgan
Content Editor: Liana Robinson
Illustrators: Story 1 - Catalina Segura; Story 2 - Conor Rawson;
　　　　　　Story 3 - James Murray; Story 4 - Haeun Kang
Design: Highline Studio

http://www.seed-learning.com

ISBN: 978-1-9464-5273-3

10 9 8 7 6 5 4 3 2 1
21 20 19 18 17

Contents

Elevator Fun

a-f

Written by **Anne Taylor**
Illustrated by **Catalina Segura**

A boy, a book, and
an elevator.

An elephant and a desk.

A cat with a fan.

Five ants and an apple.

A dog in a car.

An empty elevator?

No! An angry fish!

Lots of Lemons

g-l

Written by **Anne Taylor**
Illustrated by **Conor Rawson**

Kangaroo jumps with a girl.

Look, Kangaroo! Lemons.

A lemon for the ill gorilla.

A lemon for the happy horse.

No lemons for the lion!

Lemons for Kangaroo
and the girl.

A lemon igloo!

What's My Orange?

m-r

Written by **Anne Taylor**

Illustrated by **James Murray**

An orange for Tina.
An orange for Ken.

Look! It's a moon!

No, it's a nose!

Now it's a panda.
An octopus panda!

Quiet! It's an orange queen!

Look at my orange run!

And now it's a red orange?
No! It's an apple.

Under the Sun

s-z

Written by **Anne Taylor**
Illustrated by **Haeun Kang**

Tiger is sad.

Look in the yellow box.

An umbrella! A violin!
Six yo-yos!

Look out the window.

It's Zebra and his van!

Let's sit under the umbrella.

They are happy in the sun.

Word List

Story 1

angry

ant

apple

book

boy

car

cat

desk

dog

elephant

elevator

empty

fan

fish

five

Story 2

girl

gorilla

happy

horse

igloo

ill

jump

kangaroo

lemon

lion

look

Word List

Story 3

moon

nose

octopus

orange

panda

queen

quiet

red

run

Story 4

sad

sit

sun

tiger

under

umbrella

van

violin

window

box

six

yellow

yo-yo

zebra

How to Use

The following are some ideas for ways to use the stories in this book.

Idea 1

- ★ Choose a story.
- ★ Look at the **Word List** for that story.
- ★ Find each word from the list in the story.
- ★ Then read the story.

Idea 2

- ★ Choose a story.
- ★ Look at the illustrations for the story.
- ★ Talk about the illustrations: Point and say the words you know in the illustrations.
- ★ Look for the words from the illustrations in the story while you read.

Idea 3

- ★ Choose a story.
- ★ Look at all the words with red letters in the story. Circle the words you know.
- ★ If you don't know a word, check the **Word List**.
- ★ Then read the story.
- ★ After reading, look at the words again. Can you remember the meaning of each one?

Idea 4

- ★ Choose a story.
- ★ Look at the illustration on each page: What do you see? What is happening?
- ★ Guess what you think the page will say.
- ★ Then read the page.
- ★ Repeat for every page of the story.